BASINGSTOKE
TO
SALISBURY

Vic Mitchell and Keith Smith

Cover picture: A West of England express approaches Andover Junction East box on 14th May 1955, behind no. 35003 Royal Mail. The third coach is close to the junction with the now closed 'Sprat and Winkle' line to Romsey, seen decending steeply to Andover Town beyond the telegraph pole. (R.C.Riley)

First published May 1991

ISBN 0 906520 89 4

© *Middleton Press 1991*

Design & Laser typesetting -
          Deborah Goodridge

Published by Middleton Press
Easebourne Lane
Midhurst
West Sussex
Tel: (0730) 813169

Printed & bound by Biddles Ltd,
Guildford and Kings Lynn

CONTENTS

ACKNOWLEDEGMENTS

We are grateful for the assistance received from many of the photographers mentioned in the captions and also for the help given by C.Attwell, J.H.Bird, R.Carpenter, Dr.E.Course, A.Ll.Lambert, C.G.Maggs, R.Randell, D.Salter, G.T.V.Stacey, E.Staff, N.Stanyon and our ever supportive wives.

The Southern Railway's 1932 map shows the GWR's routes with narrow lines.

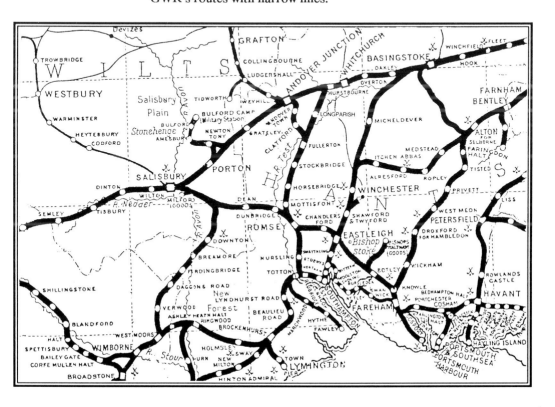

GOEGRAPHICAL SETTING

The entire route traverses the Chalk of the eastern part of Salisbury Plain, running close to the shallow valley of the infant River Test between Overton and Whitchurch. It crosses two similar valleys - that of the Bourne Rivulet, west of Hurstbourne, and the River Anton, east of Andover. Most of the remainder of the journey is in the valley of the River Bourne as far as Salisbury Tunnel, which carries the line into the Avon Valley.

The Bulford branch descended into the Bourne Valley to Newton Tony, from where it climbed over Boscombe Down before dropping steeply into the Avon Valley at Amesbury. From there the route continued at about 300ft above sea level onto Salisbury Plain at Bulford, an almost uninhabited area prior to the establishment of military camps and training areas during the Boer War.

All maps are to the scale of 25" to 1 mile, unless otherwise noted.

HISTORICAL BACKGROUND

The London & South Western Railway reached Basingstoke on 6th October 1839 and was extended to Winchester on 11th May 1840. A branch from this line to Andover was opened on 3rd July 1854, passengers to the town having to use Andover Road station (now Micheldever) until that time. Extension to Salisbury took place on 1st May 1857, trains running into the Milford terminus of the 1847 LSWR branch from Bishopstoke (Eastleigh). This involved use of what is now known as the Laverstock Loop and reversal into the station. Salisbury Tunnel and the line west to Gillingham came into use on 2nd May 1859, running parallel to the GWR's 1856 broad gauge line from Warminster for two miles. The GWR had also opened a broad gauge branch from Reading to Basingstoke in 1848.

On 3rd June 1865, the Andover & Redbridge Railway was opened by the LSWR, giving Andover a second station and a direct link to Romsey and Southampton. Andover received a further railway on 1st May 1882, when a section of the Swindon, Marlborough & Andover Railway opened. This became part of the Midland & South Western Junction Railway on 23rd June 1884, which in turn was absorbed by the GWR in 1923.

The Didcot, Newbury & Southampton Railway's trains started to pass under the route at Whitchurch in 1885 and on 1st June of that year the Hurstbourne- Fullerton line came into use.

The year 1901 saw the Basingstoke - Alton service commence on 1st June and that between Grateley and Amesbury on 1st October, for military traffic. The latter was extended to Bulford on 1st June 1906, a connection to give direct running to and from Salisbury having been opened on 7th August 1904.

Branch closures -

TO	PASSENGERS	GOODS
Alton (a)	12-9-32	30-5-36 (b)
Andover Town	7-9-64	18-9-67
Bulford	30-6-52	4-3-63
Longparish	6-7-31	28-5-56 (c)
Ludgershall	11-9-61	24-3-69 (d)

a) Closed between 1916 and 1924.
b) To Bentworth. Extremities in use until 1967.
c) Hurstbourne - Longparish closed 29th May 1934.
d) Line retained for military traffic.

The LSWR formed part of the Southern Railway in 1923, which became British Railways Southern Region in 1948. Sectorisation in 1983 resulted in the route becoming part of Network SouthEast in 1986, Southern Region finally ceasing to exist in April 1991.

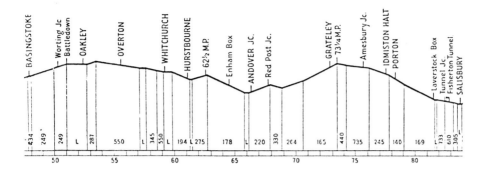

PASSENGER SERVICES

	WEEKDAYS		SUNDAYS	
	A	**B**	**A**	**B**
1869	2	3	-	3
1890	4	5	-	3
1906	5	8	-	3
1914	4	8	-	3
1924	3	9	1	2
1934	5	7	5	2
1944	5	7	5	2
1954	5	10	7	2
1964	9	7	9	-

Column A shows the number of down trains calling at principal intermediate stations between Basingstoke and Salisbury each day, while column B indicates the number of trains that stopped at most stations. Trains not included are those running on only one day of the week and those few services operating only over part of the route. For some years, these included a Waterloo - Stockbridge train on weekdays. West of England expresses are also omitted.

One consequence of the electrification of London - Bournemouth services in 1967 was the introduction of a regular interval service on the route between Basingstoke and Salisbury. On alternate hours there were trains between Waterloo and Exeter (calling at Andover) and between Basingstoke and Salisbury (calling at Andover, Grateley, Idmiston Halt and Porton). There were no stopping trains on Sundays and Whitchurch and Overton only had a few peak hour services. Subsequently, improvements restored a 2-hourly service to these stations and through running to Waterloo every hour, although this feature was largely withdrawn in January 1991, due to the lack of reliable locomotives. At this time through running of local services between Salisbury and Reading was increased from one down journey to four return trips on weekdays.

August 1934

ANDOVER JUNCTION, and SALISBURY.

Up.   Sundays.

	mrn		mrn	aft	aft	aft	aft	aft	aft	aft	**R**		aft
Salisbury...........dep.	8 10	..	9 0	2 33	5 45	32	6 14	6 22	6 39	7 38	8 12	..	9 14
Porton..................	8 22	..	..	..	5 44	..	6 32	..	..	..	..		9 24
Grateley..............	8 31	..	9 20	**R**	..	5 54	**R**	6 43	**R**	**R**	..		9 34
Andover Junc. 185......	8 50	..	9 33	..	3 29	6 6	..	7 7	..	8 58	41	..	9 44
Hurstbourne............	9 3	..	..	..	..	6 17	..	..	..	..	..		
Whitchurch **L**..........	9 10	..	..	..	..	6 23	..	..	..	8 55			9 56
Overton................	9 19	..	..	..	..	6 30	..	..	..	..			
Oakley.............[161	9 27	..	..	..	..	6 38	..	..	..	..			
Basingstoke 50,157..arr.	9 37	..	10 2	..	3 56	6 47	..	7 38	..		9 15		1013
161 Woking.........arr.	1041	...	1046	..	4 24	7 32	...	9 5	...		1037	..	11 2
161 Surbiton........ "	...		12 0	..	4 42	7 50	7 35	9 43	7 59	9	6 1010	..	1148
161 LONDON (W.).... "	...		1224	6 5	9 8	10 7	55	10 4	8 190	27	1030	..	1219

SALISBURY, ANDOVER JUNCTION, WHITCHURCH, BASINGSTOKE, and LONDON.

Up.   Week Days.

Miles																																			
	Salisbury ....dep.	7 10	8 10	9 10	8 42	9 30	10 0	1128	1133	1140	12 9	1227	1235	1 0	1 27	143	158	2 40	2 23	3 3	6 3	19	335	340	420	435	432	414	4545	3	557	635	8 8	8 55	11 0
11	Porton...............		7 19		8 54		1012		1143	1150					1101	10						345	350	420	435	350	420	435	5 15			5 9		9 5	
11	Grateley............	7 32		9 5		1024		1153	12 0	0					119	1	19					3504	0						5 25					9 16	
17½	Andover Junc. 79,184	7 41	8 35	9 17	9 57	1037		12 4	1212			1 6	130	1 29				3 8	327			4 7	410			458			5 41		7 28	36		9 29	
22½	Hurstbourne.........	7 56				1050			1215		1 39											417	429						5 52					9 40	
24½	Whitchurch **L** 51	8 2		9 30		1056		1220	1229			120	1421	1 45					339			423	425						5 58					9 46	
28	Overton.............	8 10				11 4		1228	1237			127	1	51								430	433						6 6					9 54	
31½	Oakley.......[154, 159,	8 18				1111		1235	1244			133	1	57								437	439						6 13					10 e1	
35½	Basingstoke 50,... arr.	8 28	9 2	9 49		1120		1244	1253			1422	02	6					357			446	448						6 22		7329		2	10e11	2 21
59½	159 Woking .... arr.	9 18	9 41	11640		1152		1 50					254	254	2 55					444			520	5 0						7 5		8 19	30	11 3	3 0
71½	159 Surbiton ...... "	1056	1036	1232		1413		2 33						5 6						556			615	615						7742		8189		50	12 2	3 33
83½	159 LONDON (W.) "	953	1015	1254	119	1226	0	552	0 1	41	2	32	9 3	1322	3 54	3	53	18	330	345	414	420	527	449	4556	3640	5546	7 611	6196	11 871	1730	838	101	112	30

B Arr. Woking 10 26, Surbiton 11 7, & London (Wat.) 11 1 mrn. Sats.   e 9 mins. later Weds.   **E** or **E** Mons. to Fris.   **H** Fris. (except 14th, 21st, & 28th Sept.) & Sate.

Bulford Branch

The first timetable showed six weekday trains but none on Sundays. The following examples show the rise and decline of services. Direct running to and from Grateley ceased in 1918.

July 1906

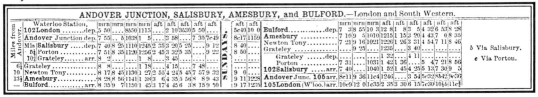

ANDOVER JUNCTION, SALISBURY, AMESBURY, and BULFORD.—London and South Western.

July 1914

LONDON, SALISBURY, ANDOVER JUNCTION, and BULFORD.—London and South Western.

NOTES.

b Via Salisbury.
c Via Porton.
h Via Andover Junction.
i Via Porton; commencing 17th inst., leaves at 12 noon, and runs via Salisbury.
k Arrives at 3 aft. on and after 18th inst.

July 1924

LONDON, SALISBURY, AMESBURY, and BULFORD.—Southern.

BULFORD, AMESBURY, SALISBURY, and LONDON.—Southern.

NOTES.

a Arrives at 4 6 aft. on Saturdays.
c Via Porton.

May 1944

LONDON, SALISBURY, AMESBURY, and BULFORD

‡ Via Porton. Dep 9 0 aft on Sats. via Salisbury. L Via Porton.

September 1951

Table 61 — LONDON, SALISBURY, AMESBURY, and BULFORD

L Via Porton.

BASINGSTOKE

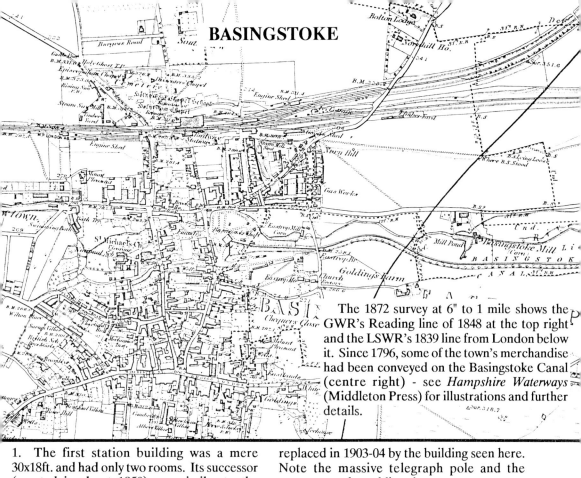

The 1872 survey at 6" to 1 mile shows the GWR's Reading line of 1848 at the top right and the LSWR's 1839 line from London below it. Since 1796, some of the town's merchandise had been conveyed on the Basingstoke Canal (centre right) - see *Hampshire Waterways* (Middleton Press) for illustrations and further details.

1. The first station building was a mere 30x18ft. and had only two rooms. Its successor (erected in about 1850) was similar to the present station at Micheldever and was replaced in 1903-04 by the building seen here. Note the massive telegraph pole and the entrance to the public subway - centre. (D.Cullum coll.)

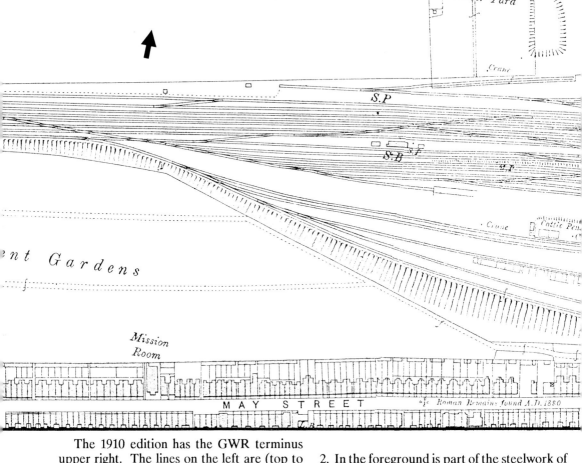

nt Gardens

Mission Room

MAY STREET

Roman Remains found A.D. 1880

The 1910 edition has the GWR terminus upper right. The lines on the left are (top to bottom) siding, Park Prewett Hospital line (from 1914), up slow, up fast, down fast, down slow, Alton line and siding. Private sidings were later provided on the north side of the yard for Eli Lilly & Co and for Tagart, Morgan & Cole.

2. In the foreground is part of the steelwork of Chapel Street bridge, which had been widened in 1875 and again in 1903. The down through and local platforms are seen, a van being visible in the down bay, which was used by Alton trains until 1916 and from 1924 until 1932. (Lens of Sutton)

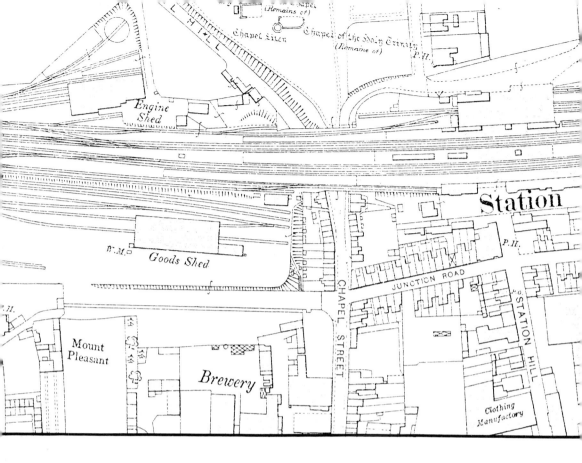

3. Being a railway cross roads, Basingstoke has long handled trains between the South Coast and the North of England. Ex-LNWR stock is running south as a special behind SR class S11 no. 404 on 7th July 1926, the spacious goods shed being evident on the right. The pneumatically operated signals were in use from 1906 until 20th November 1966. (H.C.Casserley)

4. The Bournemouth to Newcastle service on 17th August 1929 was composed of LNER stock and hauled by SR no. 663, one of the ten members of the X6 class. A horse box stands alongside the engine shed, the tall chimney to the left of it being that of the sand drier. (H.C.Casserely)

5. On the same day, U class 2-6-0 no. A613 waits to depart for Salisbury. When the platforms were widened in 1903, the population of the town was under 10,000. Such generous dimensions were fortuitous, as Basingstoke was declared a "New Town" in 1952, since which time the figures have increased from 17,000 to 144,000. (H.C.Casserley)

6. From 1947 until 1954, the station witnessed the passing of the prestigious "Devon Belle". On Saturdays in the summer of 1954 for example, it left Waterloo at noon, called at Wilton to change locomotives, and ran fast to Sidmouth Junction. It then called at principal stations to Ilfracombe, where arrival was due at 5.27pm. (H.N.James)

7. On 14th October 1962, the local service to and from Woking was operated by Hampshire DEMU no. 1107. Nearly 30 years later, part of the previous station (from about 1850) still survived on platform 4 - note the low inclined canopy on the left. (A.E.Bennett)

8. On the last weekend of September 1987, the superb Basingstoke Railshow was staged in the goods yard, which had closed in 1968. In the up siding we see nos. 70198 and 33027, while nos. 20064, 9019 and 25144 are displayed with travelling post office stock in the foreground. The 08.08 Manchester Piccadily to Weymouth service is leaving platform 2. (V.Mitchell)

9. Other exhibits at the Railshow included nos. 58005, 56065, D9000, 47581, 97403, D4, D213, D7018, 31268, 27059, 97201, 86401 and 1502. The event will be remembered by thousands for the diversity of locomotives and trade stands. (V.Mitchell)

10. Passenger figures rose from 1.8m in 1982 to 2.5m in 1984, justifying the expenditure of £100,000 on station improvements in 1985. In 1986, a £1m scheme was announced, the effects of this on the exterior being seen in September 1988. (J.Scrace)

Points for Railway Travellers.

TAKE YOUR TICKET IN ADVANCE. Tickets available for a journey from London will be despatched by post, to an applicant, by the Cashier of the Booking Office at any of the various London termini of the Company, on receipt by him of a remittance for the value of the tickets, with particulars and date of the proposed journey. These tickets may also be obtained on personal application at any of the London or Suburban Stations.

LUGGAGE IN ADVANCE. By sending their Luggage in Advance passengers avoid the inconvenience which would be experienced when taking Luggage with them.

Charge for each package, to any destination in Great Britain (other than on the London Passenger Transport Board):—

Collection, Conveyance, AND Delivery .. .. 2 -
Collection and Conveyance, OR Conveyance and Delivery 1/-

6d. extra to or from the Isle of Man and 1/- from Jersey or Guernsey.

The Charges cover Collection from and/or Delivery to addresses within the ordinary radius at Stations at which Cartage Services are in operation.

The usual Excess Luggage charges are payable in addition to the charge for each package if the total weight of Luggage per passenger exceeds 150 lbs. 1st class, 100 lbs. 3rd class.

A Consignment Note (obtainable at any Railway Station) must be filled in, and Railway Tickets produced. Tickets can be purchased in advance.

1938

BASINGSTOKE SHED

11. The shed came into use in 1905 and replaced a small single road structure on the other side of the main line. Its normal allocation was about 20 engines and on 7th July 1926 we see class T1 no. 10 and class T9 no. E721, with class O2 no. 204 under the hoist. (H.C.Casserley)

12. On 13th June 1931, the shed contained nos. E577, 585, 569 and 560. Class A12 0-4-2 no. E601 is on the eastbound train. The shed provided locomotives for local goods services and stopping trains, usually retaining one spare engine in steam for replacing defective main line engines. (H.C.Casserley)

13. No. E601 is seen more closely on the same day, with cemetery buildings in the background. This 55ft hand operated turntable was superseded by a 70ft vacuum operated one in 1942. It was moved from Portsmouth to a site west of the shed. (H.C.Casserley)

14. No. 34013 *Okehampton* passes the sand drier on 5th September 1966, as insulators lie in the "six-foot" as a prelude to electrification. This took place on 2nd January 1967, east of Basingstoke, and on 3rd April of that year westwards to Bournemouth. The shed closed when BR steam ceased on 9th July of that year. (R.E.Ruffell)

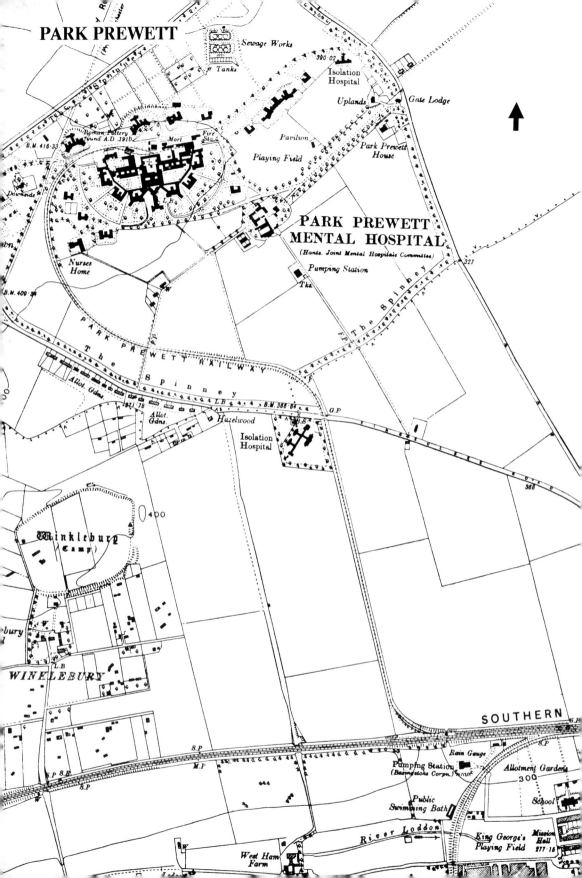

The Basingstoke - Salisbury line runs from right to left across this 1933 6" scale map. The 1.3 mile long hospital line was an extension of one of Basingstoke's sidings and had loops at the point of divergence from the main line and at the terminus. It was first used in 1914 for the conveyance of building materials and subsequently it mainly carried coal. Wagons were propelled up the 1 in 53 gradient, usually by a class G6 0-6-0T, latterly twice a week. The line was little used after 1950, officially closed in 1954 and lifted in 1956. The Alton line and Thornycroft's Motor Works are at the lower edge of the map.

15. Two platforms still remain at the hospital, the route terminating at the boiler house. Regular passenger services were never operated but ambulance coaches were reputedly moved over the line during WWI. (J.R.Fairman)

SOUTH WEST OF BASINGSTOKE

16. The main line to the West of England curves southwards between Basingstoke and Worting Junction, where it diverges west from the Southampton route. The down Southampton line is on the left. The 12.06 Salisbury to Waterloo service passes Worting Junction Box on 25th July 1964, hauled by no. 34079 *141 Squadron*. The box was in use from 30th May 1897 until 20th November 1966. Its companion at Winklebury, one mile to the east, opened on the same day but closed on 20th March 1932. (E.Wilmshurst)

17. The previous picture was taken from an occupation overbridge - this one was shot from the other side of it, nearly 20 years later. An impressive collection of station signs adds colour to the garden of one of the former railway cottages. No. 33108 is hauling a 4TC set on a Waterloo to Salisbury service. (J.Petley)

18. Comparison with the picture before last shows some of the track rearrangement that took place in 1976, including the 90mph turnouts. The crossover by the leading van was for emergency use and was operated from a ground frame after the signal box closure. No. 33059 was in charge of the Eastleigh - Clapham Yard parcels service on 24th May 1986. (D.Brown)

19. The up Southampton line passes over the Salisbury tracks on this bow-string girder structure, which came into use in May 1897, together with the quadrupled tracks east-wards. Until 1925, Battledown signal box was located to the left of the structure. No. 50005, with the 10.20 Exeter St. Davids to Waterloo service, hurries past the speed limit sign, which applies to Southampton-bound trains. (M.Turvey)

20. The 16.20 Reading to Salisbury emerges from under Battledown Flyover on 22nd August 1990. It is passing a whistle sign board for a footpath crossing as it runs onto level track, after having climbed at 1 in 249 from Basingstoke, and resumes a westerly course. (P.Barnes)

OAKLEY

21. The station opened with the line but was an early casualty, closing entirely on 17th June 1963. This view towards Basingstoke features the dangerous drops in the platforms, eliminated by the time the next photograph was taken. (Lens of Sutton)

This is the 1937 map. No changes had occured since the 1896 survey.

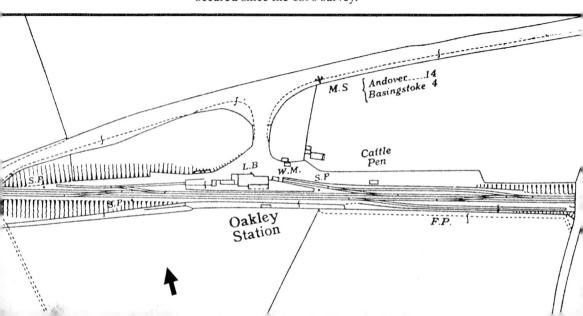

22. Although sadly not sharp, this photograph includes all three sidings, wagons in all of them and the LSWR's unusual throw-face ground signals. (Lens of Sutton)

23. Photographed on the 29th May 1966, the small signal box remained in use until 20th November of that year. The sidings had been lifted during the previous year and cable ducts set into the down platform. (C.L.Caddy)

24. The edge of the down platform was still visible on 22nd August 1990 as no. 50044 *Exeter* roared through with the 06.45 from Exeter St. Davids, complete with the new regulation headlight. Most services on this route were hauled by class 50s from May 1980. (P.Barnes)

25. The building remained in good order, in 1991 complete with its original slate roof. Remarkably, Oakley in Bedfordshire was almost exactly the same distance from its London terminus - 53 miles compared with 52½ miles. (C.Hall)

OVERTON

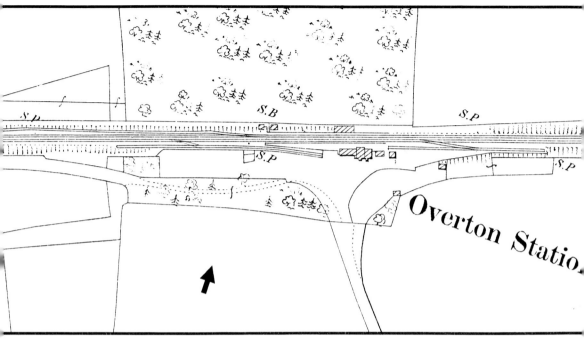

The 1896 edition marks a layout similar to that at Oakley, but in reverse as road access was from the south.

26. The efforts of the architect who designed such elaborate barge boards were somewhat negated by later sanitary and telegraph engineers. The wooden additions had little to commend them aesthetically. (Lens of Sutton)

27. A deep chalk cutting is visible in the distance, one of a large number on the route. A train was snowbound in one nearby for several days in 1926. Note the absence of a foot crossing at this station. (Lens of Sutton)

The 1938 survey includes Portal's private siding and a footbridge between the platforms. Henri de Portal, a Huguenot refugee, was awarded a contract to manufacture banknote paper for the Bank of England in 1724, a franchise held by Portals ever since.

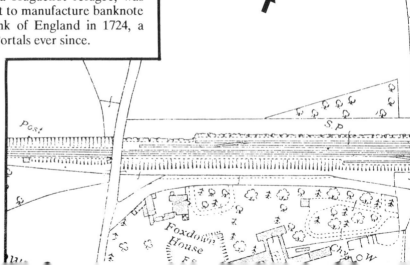

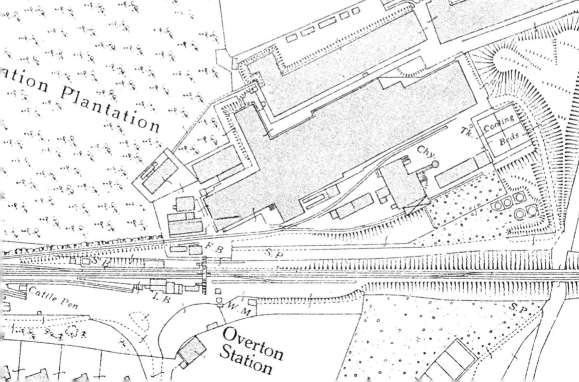

28. Both a barrow crossing and a footbridge were eventually provided, the latter having been the eastern footbridge at Yeovil Junction until 1920. The station opened with the line but the goods yard closed on 5th July 1965. In 1938, it was listed as having a crane of 5-ton capacity. (Lens of Sutton)

29. The signal box, seen in May 1966, was closed on 5th February 1967, after which date access to the remaining up siding for engineers trains was by ground frame. By January 1991, the former had gone but the latter remained. The source of the River Test is one mile south of the station and the line follows the infant river to Whitchurch. Passenger traffic has never been heavy - the local population was under 1500 for the first 50 years of the station and is now only about 4000.
(C.L.Caddy)

30. Staffing ceased in January 1969 but recently tickets have been obtainable from the kiosk on the left, in the morning peak hours. No. 50045 *Achilles* makes a brief stop with the 09.00 Yeovil Junction to Waterloo train on 22nd August 1990. (P.Barnes)

WHITCHURCH

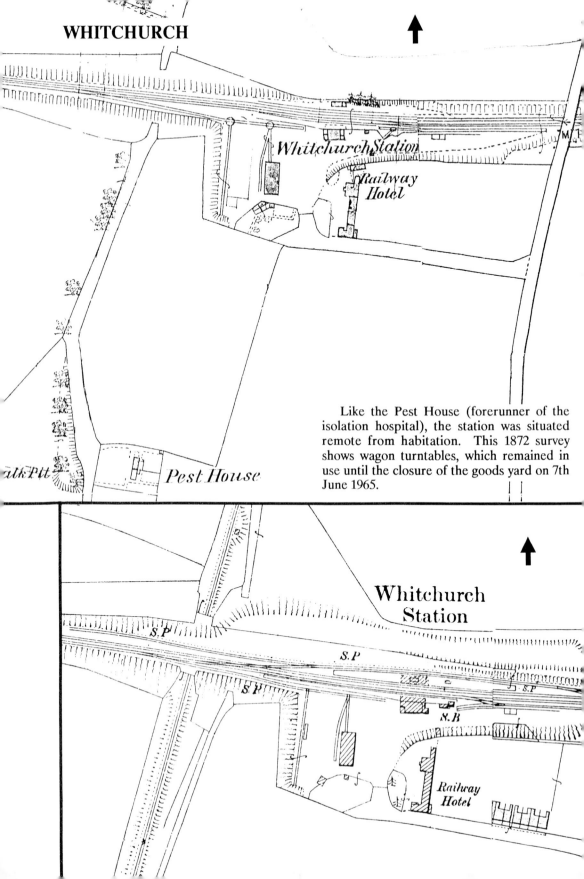

Whitchurch Station

Railway Hotel

Pest House

alk Ptt

Like the Pest House (forerunner of the isolation hospital), the station was situated remote from habitation. This 1872 survey shows wagon turntables, which remained in use until the closure of the goods yard on 7th June 1965.

Whitchurch Station

S.P

S.P

S.P

S.P

S.B

Railway Hotel

31. The original building from 1854 is on the left, while the curved canopy dates from 1885. Few of the LSWR wooden footbridges of this type have survived - an exception is at Farnham. Whitchurch Silk Mill, which still produces legal and academic silk, once sent its products by rail. (Lens of Sutton)

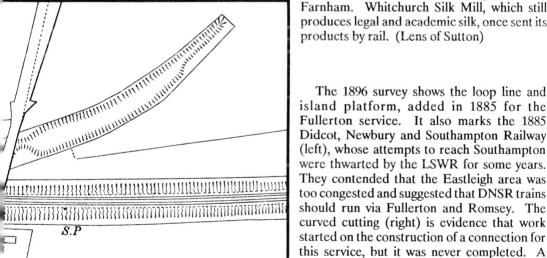

S.P

Allotment Gardens

The 1896 survey shows the loop line and island platform, added in 1885 for the Fullerton service. It also marks the 1885 Didcot, Newbury and Southampton Railway (left), whose attempts to reach Southampton were thwarted by the LSWR for some years. They contended that the Eastleigh area was too congested and suggested that DNSR trains should run via Fullerton and Romsey. The curved cutting (right) is evidence that work started on the construction of a connection for this service, but it was never completed. A second siding over the DNSR line was added later.

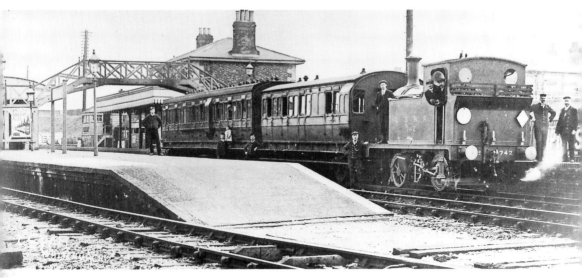

32. A Fullerton-bound train awaits departure behind no. 742, which operated this service from 1906 until 1911. It was one of ten 2-2-0s built as class C14 for lines with minimal traffic. The DNSR station was over one mile to the south and closed in 1960. (Lens of Sutton)

34. On the left of this May 1966 view are the remains of the Fullerton loop. It had been downgraded to a siding in August 1939 and was finally taken out of use in December 1966. The steel footbridge was erected in 1923. (C.L.Caddy)

33. Fullerton services were withdrawn in 1931 but the station continues to serve the local community which has grown from about 2000, when the line opened, to 4000 today. The exterior has changed little over the years and is seen in July 1963. (H.C.Casserley)

35. Another 1966 view shows the cattle dock and the east end points, shortly before they were removed. The signal box closed on 5th February 1967, when colour light signals were introduced. The station was renamed Whitchurch North on 26th September 1949 and Whitchurch (Hants) on 2nd October 1972. (C.L.Caddy)

36. No. D802 *Formidable* is westbound on 29th May 1966, these class 42 locomotives being in use on the route between 1964 and 1971. The new cable duct had recently been laid on the bed of the goods shed siding, which had been last used in 1965. (C.L.Caddy)

37. On 6th August 1966, no. 34013 *Okehampton* passed through, bound for Clapham Junction with a troop special from Salisbury. Platform gas lighting was still evident, although the locomotive was equipped with electric. (S.C.Nash)

38. The finer features of the stanchion brackets on the down platform are probably overlooked by most passengers. Progressive raising of the track has meant that the platform has had to follow. In 1984, the slope towards the doorway had become so great that a retaining wall was added inside the posts and a ramp provided. (C.Hall)

39. The goods shed was unusual in being at right angles to the main line. This is the south elevation of the structure, which was demolished in 1990 to make way for larger commericial premises. (C.Hall)

40. No. 56034 *Castell Ogwr / Ogmore Castle* races through on 19th September 1988, with stone from Whatley Quarry to Woking, where a terminal had recently been established in the down yard. All the buildings were still standing in 1991 and the booking office was staffed on weekday mornings. (J.Scrace)

HURSTBOURNE

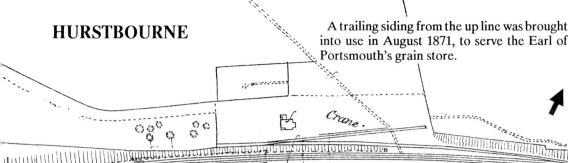

A trailing siding from the up line was brought into use in August 1871, to serve the Earl of Portsmouth's grain store.

Crane.

M.P. London 61

Hurstbourne Siding

41. The Board of Trade Inspector reported on the state of progress of the new station on 8th December 1882. He said that he was reasonably satisfied with the work but he questioned the lack of a toilet on the down platform. He felt that passengers would not have time to cross over the line to the other platform to use the toilet there while the train waited in the station. It was pointed out that facilities were available at Basingstoke, that very few trains would stop at Hurstbourne and that those that did would not stop for long enough for anyone to use the toilet, even if there was one on the down platform. Colonel Holland reluctantly agreed with this arrangement and allowed the station to remain open. Traffic had commenced on the 1st of the month. The 5-ton crane and the signal box are in the distance. (Lens of Sutton)

The 1896 survey shows the full extent of the goods yard, which closed on 6th May 1963 and is now occupied by a scrap metal merchant.

Tank

it Dwellings (Site of)

S.P. *S.B.*

S.P.

F.P.

S.P.

Hurstbourne Station

42. On 1st June 1906, class H13 steam railcar no. 12 was introduced on the Whitchurch-Fullerton service, but was popular with neither staff nor passengers and was withdrawn from this service in 1910. The sub-structure of the platform is evident in this view from about 1908. (Lens of Sutton)

43. A westward view reveals that both platforms were of timber construction and that there was a covered approach to the up platform. The signal box, behind the camera, was damaged by fire in 1954 but remained in use until 15th June 1964. Passenger facilities were withdrawn on 6th April of that year. (Lens of Sutton)

44. The 10.15 Salisbury to Basingstoke stopping train crosses Hurstbourne Viaduct on 22nd January 1967 and approaches the site of the station, which was just beyond the right border of the picture. Watercress from beds on the far side of the viaduct once provided substantial railway revenue. The Bourne River supplied fresh water from chalk springs. (J.Scrace)

45. By 1966, there was little evidence of Hurstbourne Junction, which was just off the left border of the previous picture. The double track branch, which passed through the left arch, was singled on 13th July 1913. Passenger services ceased on 6th July 1931 and the line to Longparish closed completely on 29th May 1934. The route from Longparish southwards is featured in our *Andover to Southampton* album. (H.C.Casserley)

46. The preserved "Merchant Navy", no. 35028 *Clan Line*, crosses the Anton Valley, as it approaches Andover on 27th April 1974, with a railtour. Until 14th October 1934, an intermediate signal box had been in use at Enham. (J.Scrace)

ANDOVER JUNCTION

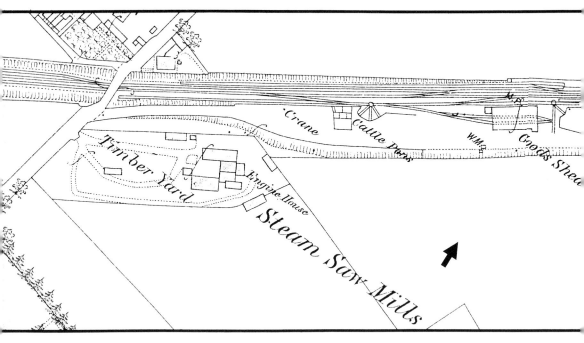

The 1873 survey marks the position of the first engine shed (which was destroyed by fire in 1899) and has the then single line to Andover Town lower right. A later edition appears in our *Andover to Southampton* album, along with other photographs.

47. The main building of 1854 remains little altered today, but the platforms were drastically rearranged in 1882 when the line from Marlborough reached Andover, whereas a bay platform had sufficed for the 1865 Romsey line. (Pamlin Prints)

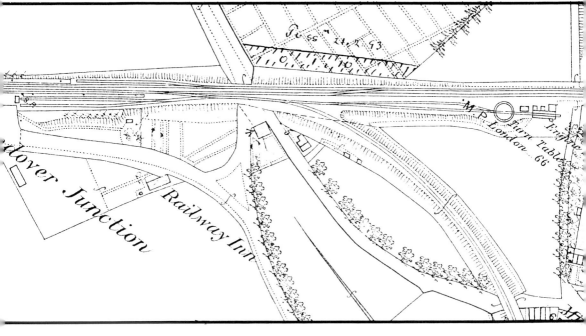

48. In 1882, the up platform was rebuilt further north, allowing two through lines to be added. A down freight train snakes over the connection on 16th September 1899. The up through line was not so sharply curved and was therefore of value to non-stop passenger trains. (Lens of Sutton)

49. The up platform (right) was rebuilt as an island, its outer face being used mainly by SMAR trains. On 3rd April 1928 4-4-0 no. 0478 passes West Box, one of two provided in 1882, their predecessor having been situated on the down platform. (H.C.Casserley)

50. U class no. 1633 accelerates a westbound train, while GWR no. 2251 waits to leave with a northbound service, in about 1938. The GWR absorbed the route to Marlborough, Swindon and Cheltenham in 1923. (C.R.L.Coles)

51. A stopping train departs towards Basingstoke, shortly before WWII. No. 598 is one of the A12 "Jubilee" class. Andover Junction is the background while, on the left, we see one of three sidings that remained in use until 1965. This was the site of the first engine shed. (C.R.L.Coles)

52. On 2nd June 1952, the down yard was being shunted by class T9 no. 30284, originally used on prestigious express passenger services. Behind it is the yard's 7½-ton capicity crane, the cattle pens and McDougall's flour mills. (S.C.Nash)

53. A down stopping service departs on 14th May 1955, behind no. 30779 *Sir Colgrevance*, one of the successful "King Arthur" class. Later known as "B Box", the signal box, along with its companion (visible in the next picture), remained in use until 2nd December 1973. (R.C.Riley)

54. Viewed on the same day is the goods shed (right), the water accommodation showing evidence of extension to meet the demands of this once expanding station. The suffix "Junction" was in use from 1865 until 1964. Note that the former down through line had become a siding. (R.C.Riley)

55. U class no. 31634 arrives with a terminating freight service in May 1955. Near the bridge in the distance, a ground frame controlled the points from the down goods yard. (R.C.Riley)

56. Until the mid-1930s, Andover saw through services between Southampton and the North of England, but by the time this photograph was taken on 6th April 1957, the most northerly destination was Cheltenham. This is the 2.35pm local service to Swindon Town, the GWR having operated the route since 1923. (N.Sprinks)

58. The disused cattle dock is in the right foreground as no. D805 heads west with the 13.10 from Waterloo on 23rd July 1969. The double span of the goods shed roof was unusual - another large shed had been in use at Andover Town until 1967. (J.Scrace)

←

57. September 10th 1961 was the last day of public operation of the ex-MSWJR line and the 12.40pm departure was inexplicably composed of one ER corridor, one MR corridor and two WR compartment coaches, hauled by nos. 6395 and 6327. Two sidings separate the single line to Swindon from the double tracks of the Salisbury route. (J.J.Smith)

59. The 09.40 from Exeter St. Davids approaches Andover on 4th March 1982, having passed the grain silo (in the background), which had a private siding from 1943 until 1962. Through the right arch passes the former MSWJR line, which in 1991 still remained in use for military traffic as far as Ludgershall, carrying one train on most working days. (A.Dasi-Sutton)

60. Ex-SDJR 2-8-0 no. 53809 waits to leave for Ludgershall on 26th September 1987, with a special train from the Basingstoke Railshow, which had been brought in by no. 37116 (left). The 10-lever ground frame is visible nearby. (P.Barnes)

61. The curved extensions to the up platform canopy were still evident in 1988, the bay for the trains to Andover Town, Fullerton and Romsey having been adjacent to the distant one. Like Basingstoke, Andover became an "overspill town", its 1901 population of 6500 rising to 26,000 in 1971 and to nearly 100,000 in 1990. (J.Scrace)

62. The large building in the background was opened as a fertiliser depot in May 1969 and continues to have its own siding, visible at the far end of the up platform. The siding receives one or two train loads of bagged fertiliser per month and an occasional tanker of limejuice from Italy. Chipman's weed control train is seen in action on 13th April 1990, with Hunslet-Barclay no. 20901 *Nancy* near the camera and no. 20904 *Lorna* at the far end. The down goods sidings had been lifted in 1985, following despatch of a load of wheat to Glasgow Docks on 6th March. The last parcel vans left the goods shed on 25th September 1980 and the last mail vans followed on 28th May 1981. One addition in 1985 was installation of the points to the left of the up waiting room. (D.Brown)

ANDOVER SHEDS

63. The former MSWJR shed is on the right and the 1904 LSWR shed is on the left, both being on the present site of the UKF fertiliser depot. Visible between them on 30th April 1928 are the white walls of the turntable pit. (H.C.Casserley)

64. Ex-MSWJR no. 1336 had just been turned when photographed on 9th May 1953, having worked a railtour over its old company's route. The 50ft. turntable was provided by the MSWJR but was eventually shared with the LSWR. (N.Sprinks)

65. The Western Region continued to use the former MSWJR shed until 1958 but the ex-LSWR one was not abandoned until 1962. One of Beattie's 2-4-0 WTs is being prepared for the 2.28 pm railtour to Bulford Camp on 14th May 1955. (J.H.Aston)

RED POST JUNCTION

66. A separate single line for MSWJR trains was provided, except for the first six months of operation in 1882. Class H15 no.334 approaches the junction with a Salisbury- bound train. Between 1901 and 1919 there were 22 automatic pneumatic signals controlling 12 sections between here and Grateley.
(Lens of Sutton)

RED POST JCT

67. During both World Wars, connections were provided here between the Salisbury and Swindon lines. During WWII, the line to Weyhill was doubled and remained so until 28th August 1960, both double tracks running parallel for a short distance. The driver of a Cheltenham to Southampton freight is about to accept the tablet for the single line to Andover Junction on 14th May 1955.
(R.C.Riley)

68. The signal box was in use from 5th September 1943 to 1st September 1963, although it had not controlled the Weyhill line since 1960. Between 1919 and 1937, a block post had been located in the V of the junction, this also controlling a loop on the Weyhill route and two crossovers to the SR main line. The 2.50pm from Andover Junction to Swindon is about to turn north on 27th August 1960.
(J.J.Smith)

GRATELEY

Right is the 1896 map showing the layout before the major widening and alterations of 1901. Below is the 1910 survey, the upper line on the left being the 1902 single track to Amesbury and the upper one on the right being a long siding. The private siding, south of the station, was for the Marquis of Winchester's estate, the short siding north of the station on the 1896 edition probably being its predecessor.

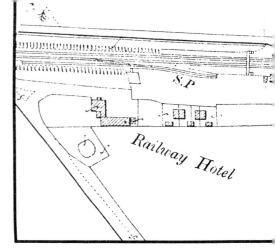

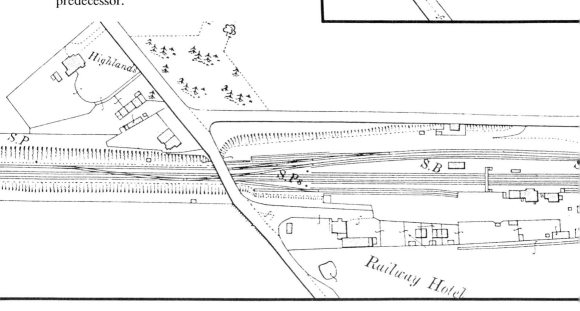

69. The station opened on 1st May 1857, when the village had only about 150 inhabitants. The island platform was built to serve the Amesbury branch trains, which started to carry the public on 2nd June 1902. The short dock siding (lower left) was removed in 1946 but the other was usable until 1964. (Lens of Sutton)

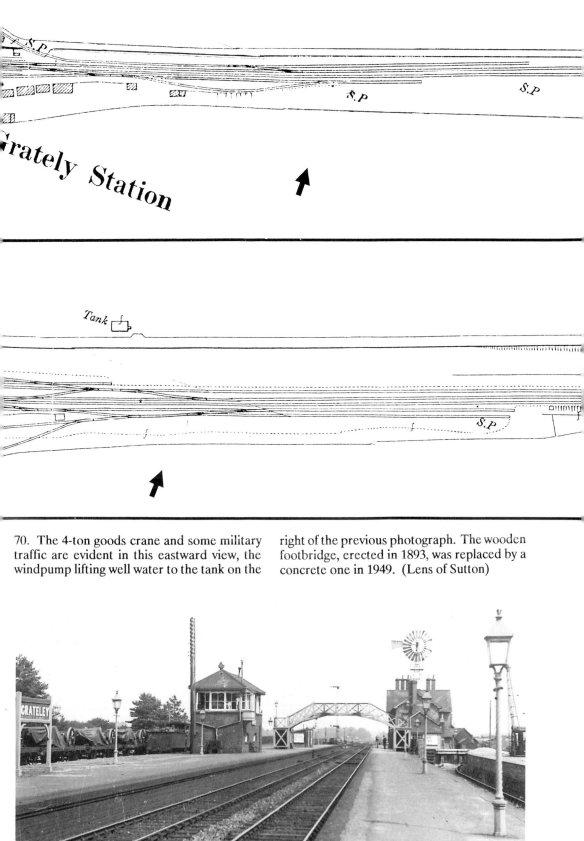

rately Station

Tank

70. The 4-ton goods crane and some military traffic are evident in this eastward view, the windpump lifting well water to the tank on the right of the previous photograph. The wooden footbridge, erected in 1893, was replaced by a concrete one in 1949. (Lens of Sutton)

Early Pneumatic Signalling

The installation at Grately used air at 7lb. pressure for the controls to and from the signalbox, and a pressure of 15lb. was used for the movement of the points and signals. A feature not met with elsewhere in Great Britain was that the signals were replaced to danger by air pressure, and not by gravity alone. The lever frame in the signalbox consisted of a row of pull-handles operating air slide-valves. To reverse a pair of points, the signalman pulled (or pushed) the corresponding slide about 3/4 of its stroke, to open the relay valves at the points, and admit air at 15lb. pressure to the mechanism, which threw and relocked the points. If these operations were completed correctly, an air message at 7lb. pressure returned to the signalbox, and operated a valve which completed the stroke of the lever slide. No such indicating action took place when a signal was cleared, but did so when it was returned to danger. The two chief disadvantages of the system were the time taken to transmit the controls by air to points and signals at a considerable distance from the signalbox, and that if the points failed to complete their stroke, special measures had to be taken to restore them to their original position. The second defect was overcome subsequently. On the LSWR, the drawbacks inseparable from the "all air" system were overcome by the adoption of the electropneumatic system, but the installations at Grateley were replaced by mechanical signalling. Automatic intermediate signals to Red Post Junction had also been in use until that time. The objectives of long range operation and labour reduction had been achieved but track circuiting could not be incorporated directly and so eventually electric colour light signalling was adopted as a preferable automatic system.

71. The signal box housed a prototype pneumatic frame from 1901 to 1919. It was shorter than normal, as the levers were at 3ins. centres, instead of the usual 5ins. used in mechanical boxes, and they performed more than one function, reducing the number required from 87 to 72. The projection on the left was for observation, while that on the right housed the toilet - a late addition. (C.L.Caddy)

72. Class M7 no. 30108 returns with the last passenger carrying train from Bulford on 23rd March 1963, scheduled services on the branch having ceased in 1952. On the right is part of the vast tonnage of point rodding that had to be moved after the effortless pneumatic system had been abandoned, owing to the high cost of improvements. (R.E.Ruffell)

73. No. 34032 *Camelford* hauls coaches of "blood and custard" livery, which replaced the traditional all green paintwork in the 1950s. The signal post diamonds indicated the presence of track circuits. The long span steel bridge dated from the 1901 widening works. (D.Cullum coll.)

74. The goods yard closed to traffic on 10th June 1963 but the booking office was staffed until 5th October 1969. The LCGB's "Green Arrow Rail Tour" heads west on 3rd July 1966, behind no. 34002 *Salisbury*. The vestigial mechanical signalling ceased to function on 2nd May 1968. (J.Scrace)

75. No. 33102 failed at Grateley on 17th March 1988, while working the 10.10 Waterloo to Salisbury service. No. 47306 arrived wrong line from Salisbury to rescue the stranded train from this now featureless location. Although the population of the village has risen to only 520, the station is used by people from a large district. (J.Scrace)

76. Privately owned no. 59003 *Yeoman Highlander* works a few empties from Woking to Merehead Quarry on 17th August 1990. The powerful class 59s had only just started to operate this service regularly. A batch of four were built in the USA in 1985 and were fitted with 16-cylinder engines generating 3300hp. (D.Brown)

77. For over two miles west of Grateley, the Bulford branch single track ran parallel to the main lines. It had been little used by passenger trains after direct running from the branch to Salisbury became possible in 1904, but it continued to carry freight services until 4th March 1963. It is visible on the left, as 1954-built 1-Co-Co-1 diesel-electric no. 10203 speeds west on 14th May 1955. (N.Sprinks)

BULFORD BRANCH

The 1913 revision of the 1" to 1 mile survey shows the branch leaving the main line (lower right), the junction details being shown on the next map. A single line between Grateley and Amesbury was opened for military traffic on 1st October 1901, for general goods service on 26th April 1902 and to public passengers on 2nd June of that year. Double track to Amesbury came into use on 7th August 1904. Minimisation of legal costs was the main reason for the Amesbury & Military Camp Light Railway having been built by the LSWR under a Light Railway Order. Economies in signalling and track specification were allowed under these provisions but were not practised in this case. South of Amesbury, a short branch is shown to Boscombe Down Camp, it being well used during 1917-18 for airfield construction materials. Beyond Amesbury, the line was single to Bulford and was opened on 1st June 1906. A military line branched off at Ratfyn and can be seen to serve camps at Larkhill, Durrington, Rollestone and others in the Stonehenge area. Beyond Bulford the line continues to Bulford Camp (marked *PLATFORM*) and Sling Plantation.

AMESBURY JUNCTION

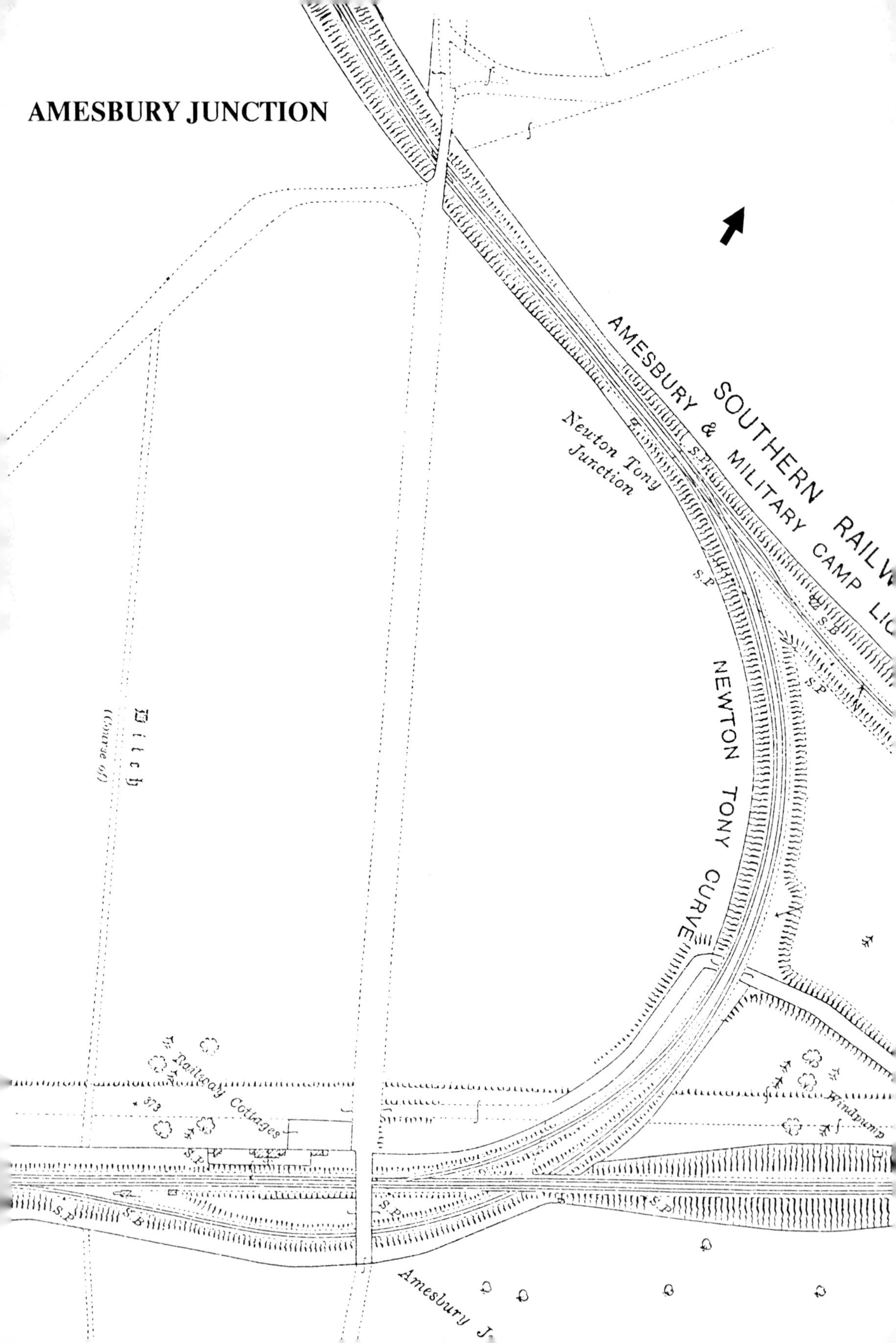
AMESBURY & MILITARY CAMP LI
SOUTHERN RAILW
Newton Tony Junction
S.P.
S.B
NEWTON TONY CURVE
Ditch (Course of)
Railway Cottages
373
Windpump
Amesbury J

78. Looking towards Grateley, the route of the former down line from Bulford is on the right, the up line once diverging left, beyond the bridge. The signal box was renamed Allington on 30th June 1952, when branch passenger services ceased. (Lens of Sutton)

The 1925 map has the 1901 single track to Grateley on the right of the triangle and the 1904 double track connection on the left. The Roman Road is parallel to the main line for over three miles. Allington Box closed on 20th January 1964.

P O R T   W A Y
R O M A N   R O A D
(From Old Sarum to Silchester)
3ª 2·541

OUTHERN RAILWAY
SINGSTOKE & SALISBURY

NEWTON TONY

79. The down platform originally had the signal box adjacent to the small corrugated iron clad building. The lean-to on the end was for the gents and the curved-roof building was for goods. (Lens of Sutton)

80. This view of the up platform shows the later position of the signal box and that buildings on both platforms were finished with pebble-dash. Until October 1903, the name was spelt "Newton Toney". (Lens of Sutton)

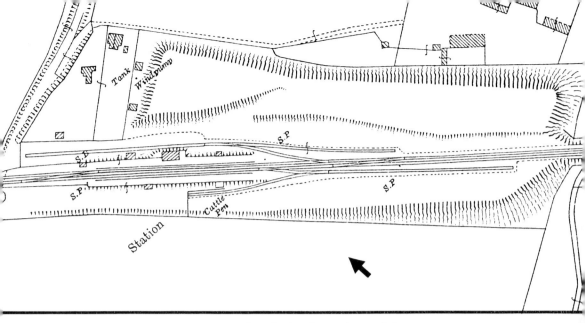

The 1925 map has the level crossing and the
line to Amesbury on the left.

81. A 1955 picture includes a felled signal post and shows that two were retained to protect the level crossing gates, the only ones on the branch. The line to Amesbury was singled on 25th October 1953 and that to Newton Tony Junction followed on 17th October 1954. At this time the track was slewed between the platforms to link the two remaining single lines. (N.Sprinks)

AMESBURY

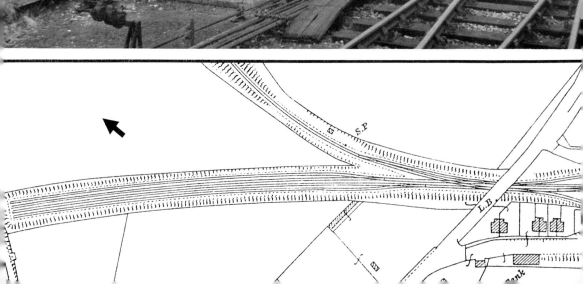

82. The down platform (left) appears to be well established but the up shelter is having its guttering fitted. The photograph therefore probably dates from extension of the station at the time of the opening of the Bulford line in 1906. (Lens of Sutton)

84. Looking towards Newton Tony from the footbridge in 1928, we can appreciate how much the cutting was widened to accommodate two short sidings. The two nearest platforms were signalled for the departure of up passenger trains but military trains could be hand signalled out of the three dock roads. (H.C.Casserley)

83. Two of the military docks are visible in this view of the 24-lever signal box at the south end of the station. The docks were devoid of all features, except lamp posts, so that battalions of men could be accommodated in formation. (Lens of Sutton)

The 1924 edition has the double track from Newton Tony on the right (upper pair). On the left are the four Shrewton sidings, used for berthing troop trains. The crane (Cr.) was of 5 ton capacity. An ash pit was provided in the short siding by the turntable.

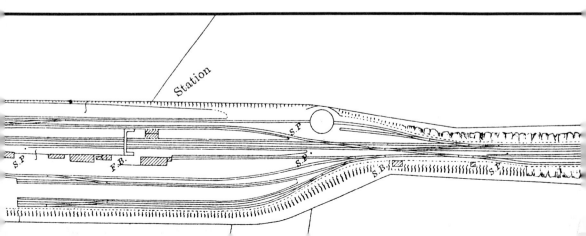

85. A 1955 photograph reveals that the up platform canopy had gone by then, but that the 1943 temporary down shelter had been retained, as had the two starting signals. The station was little used by the public, although there were nearly 5000 inhabitants at the time of closure. (S.C.Nash)

86. With the bleak windswept expanse of Salisbury Plain in the background, 2-4-0 WT no. 30587 is turned on the 45ft. turntable, after having arrived with the REC railtour on 14th May 1955. The main stores of the NAAFI was (and is) at Amesbury, generating a considerable rail traffic of military catering provisions. (J.H.Aston)

87. A glimpse south on 24th September 1960 from the then A303 road bridge includes the 10-lever ground frame. Until 1954 it contained 18 levers, having replaced a 3-lever frame in 1906. The buffer stops on the left were added in 1954 when the connection from the loop to the Bulford line was removed. (R.M.Casserley)

88. Class M7 no. 30108 had been signalled out of the up platform and is starting the long climb at 1 in 60 on 23rd March 1963, three weeks after the last goods train had left. Troop trains had often required piloting over the branch, although only the "Merchant Navy" class and the heavy 4-6-0s were banned from the line. (S.C.Nash)

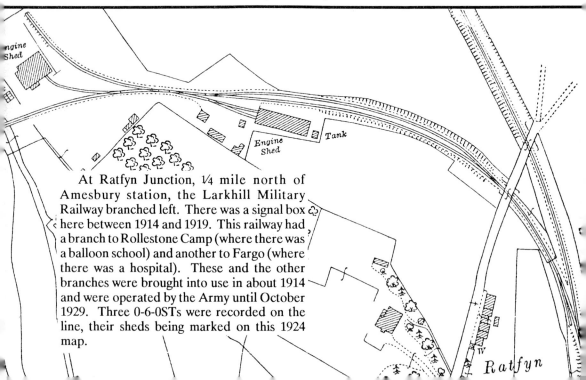

At Ratfyn Junction, ¼ mile north of Amesbury station, the Larkhill Military Railway branched left. There was a signal box here between 1914 and 1919. This railway had a branch to Rollestone Camp (where there was a balloon school) and another to Fargo (where there was a hospital). These and the other branches were brought into use in about 1914 and were operated by the Army until October 1929. Three 0-6-0STs were recorded on the line, their sheds being marked on this 1924 map.

BULFORD

89. An early postcard includes most of the goods yard, the small goods shed, and platform rolling in progress - a regular necessity prior to the advent of tarmac. (Lens of Sutton)

90. Class T1 no. E69 poses against the featureless landscape of Salisbury Plain on 28th April 1928. The water tank was filled by a windpump drawing from a well in the chalk. The signal box was demoted to a ground frame in April 1935. (H.C.Casserley)

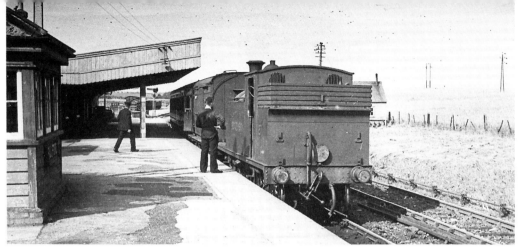

91. Two coaches were ample for the traffic offering at 6.26 pm on 12th July 1947. Class M7 no. 127 would not have been worked hard, as most passengers had deserted the railway since the bus service to Salisbury was more direct, quicker, cheaper and terminated in the city centre. (J.J.Smith)

92. Class T9 4-4-0 no. 30719 shunts the stock of the 1.0pm service from Salisbury on 2nd June 1952, four weeks before passenger services ceased. The single coach remained at Bulford overnight. The SR had replaced the original timber platform edge with precast concrete components. (S.C.Nash)

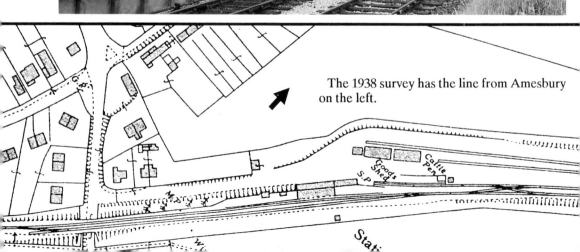

The 1938 survey has the line from Amesbury on the left.

BULFORD CAMP

93. The long desolate platform was devoid of shelter or other features and did not have a regular passenger service. This shows the REC railtour on 14th May 1955, 2-4-0WT no. 30587 having run round its three coaches.
(H.C.Casserley)

94. "The Rambling Rose" on 23rd March 1963 was the last train on the branch. Looking towards Bulford, we have a short line on the left which terminated at an end loading dock, while the track in the foreground once continued a further ¾ mile to Sling Camp.
(R.M.Casserley)

The line from Bulford Camp to the terminus passed over three ungated level crossings. This 1924 map shows the end of the line at Sling Camp, the tracks remaining in place until 1933.

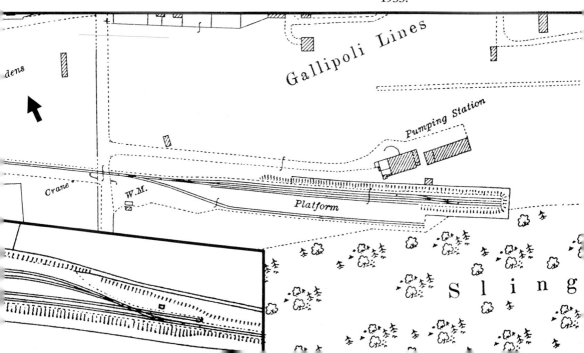

IDMISTON HALT

95. The halt was two miles west of Amesbury Junction and was opened on 3rd January 1943 to serve the nearby Porton Down Camp. One platform is visible behind the brake van of this up freight train on 12th September 1964. The locomotive is no. 30823, one of the class S15s. (S.C.Nash)

96. The buildings are on the down platform as most passengers were destined for Salisbury. The lane from Idmiston village to Porton Camp passes under the line between the second and third telegraph poles. (C.L.Caddy)

97. Concrete was the principal material for construction at another contemporary wartime halt, at Hamble. While this remains open, Idmiston was closed on 9th September 1968. (Lens of Sutton)

PORTON

98. Looking towards London, we see some of the six railway cottages built beyond the occupation bridge. The signal box had 17 levers and remained in use until 2nd May 1968, the crossover lasting until November 1967.
(Lens of Sutton)

The 1925 survey shows the extent of the narrow gauge lines at Porton Down. They were in use from about 1916 to 1946 and were mainly operated by petrol locomotives, although an 0-6-0T was listed in the early years. The location of the railway, and its southward branch, can be seen (lower left) on the 1" scale map of the Bulford Branch shown after picture 77.

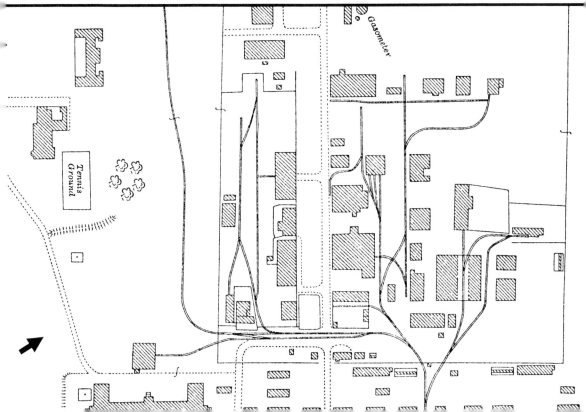

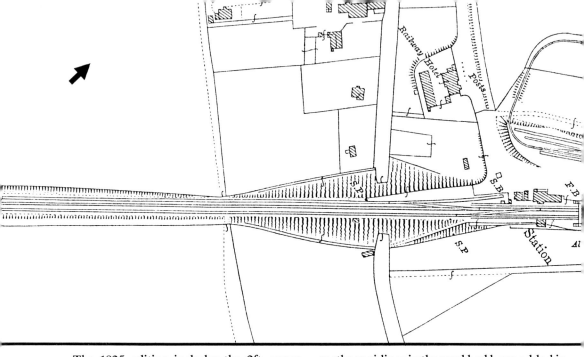

The 1925 edition includes the 2ft. gauge military railway which ran to Porton Down Camp and passed over the main line on a former farm occupation bridge. The two northern sidings in the yard had been added in 1899. The area is now occupied by a garden centre.

99. Situated high on the side of the Bourne Valley, the station was conveniently placed in relation to the small village. The original single siding is adjacent to the up platform, on the right. The 2-ton crane marked on the map was used mainly for transhipment of goods between narrow and standard gauge wagons. (D.Cullum Coll.)

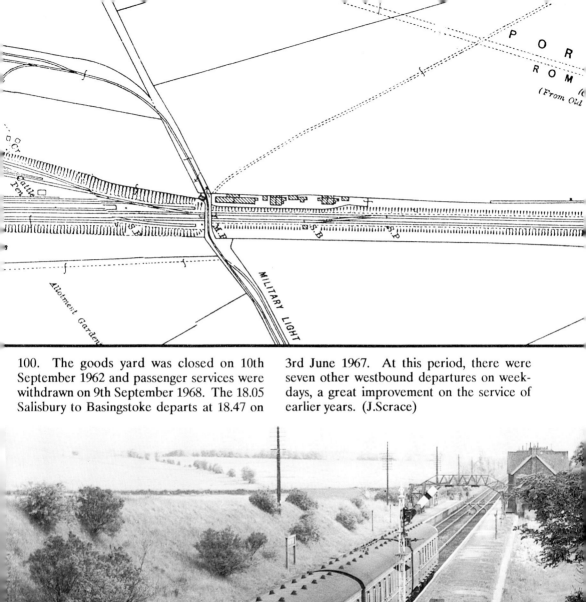

100. The goods yard was closed on 10th September 1962 and passenger services were withdrawn on 9th September 1968. The 18.05 Salisbury to Basingstoke departs at 18.47 on 3rd June 1967. At this period, there were seven other westbound departures on weekdays, a great improvement on the service of earlier years. (J.Scrace)

EAST OF SALISBURY

101. A down freight service from Basingstoke passes under the A30 London Road, as it approaches Salisbury Tunnel on 3rd April 1965, behind no. 34032 *Camelford*. The line to Romsey and Southampton is on the right. (S.C.Nash)

102. The fireman waves to the signalman of Salisbury Tunnel Junction box on 28th April 1964, as the "Atlantic Coast Express" emerges from the tunnel. Allotments are in evidence north and south of the box, which closed on 17th August 1981. It had taken over the work of Laverstock, (one mile towards London) on 16th December 1930. (E.Wilmshurst)

103. No. 50001 approaches the tunnel on 3rd August 1990 with the 12.15 from Waterloo, with the Laverstock Loop in the background. This single line was brought into use as a diversionary route on 17th August 1981, forming a triangular junction for the first time. The embankment existed, carrying a line to the Milford terminus, for two years until the tunnel was completed and the station opened on the present site on 2nd May 1859. (P.Barnes)

104. Having passed through the 443yd. long Salisbury Tunnel (also known as Fisherton or Bishop's Down Tunnel), no. 73087 approaches the station with a Portsmouth to Cardiff train on 3rd April 1965. The up Salisbury Tunnel Junction signals are partially obscured by steam but the East Yard headshunt is clearly visable, a ground frame and connection to the up line having been added in 1910. The Salisbury Ring Road bridge was built at this location in 1968. (S.C.Nash)

SALISBURY

The building marked "Terminus" on this 1937 survey had been the GWR station until 12th September 1932, when all services were transferred to the adjacent SR platforms. The first station consisted of a long platform on the down side, with a bay at the London end but ticket platforms were provided east of the station. Up trains had to wait here, much to the annoyance of passengers, until there was an opportunity to reverse into the main platform. This nonsense came to an end on 19th August 1878, when a new station for up trains was opened, *east* of Fisherton Street. A bay platform was also provided. There was direct access from the street and a subway connection to the down bay platform. This inconvenient arrangement lasted until the station was rebuilt in 1901-02, when four through platforms were provided, together with east and west bays. The 1878 up platform closed on 6th April 1902, when the new no. 1 platform came into use.

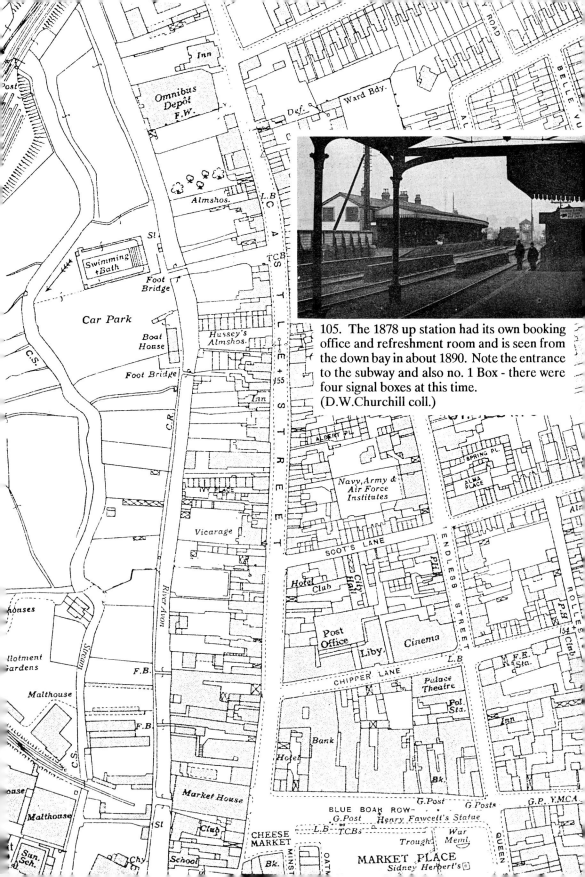

105. The 1878 up station had its own booking office and refreshment room and is seen from the down bay in about 1890. Note the entrance to the subway and also no. 1 Box - there were four signal boxes at this time. (D.W.Churchill coll.)

Map labels:

Inn

Omnibus Depôt F.W.

Ward Bdy.

Def.

BELLE VUE

Almshos.

L.B.

Swimming Bath

St.

Foot Bridge

Car Park

Boat House

Hussey's Almshos.

Foot Bridge

Tan.

TCB

155

C.S.

C.R.

River Avon

ALBERT PL.

SPRING PL.

ALMA PLACE

Navy, Army & Air Force Institutes

IVY PLACE

SCOT'S LANE

ENDLESS STREET

Vicarage

ROLLE'S...

P.O. Club

154

Hotel

Club

City Hall

P.H.

Post Office

Liby.

Cinema

L.B.

M.F.E. Sta.

CHIPPER LANE

Palace Theatre

Pol. Sta.

Inn

Bank

Hotel

Bk.

Stream

F.B.

Allotment Gardens

...houses

...lotment Gardens

Malthouse

F.B.

C.S.

Market House

St.

Club

Malthouse

BLUE BOAR ROW

G.Post G Posts

G.P. YMCA

G.Post

Henry Fawcett's Statue

CHEESE MARKET

L.B.

TCBs

Trough

War Meml.

Bk.

MINST...

OATM...

MARKET PLACE

Sidney Herbert's

Sun. Sch.

School

Chy.

QUEEN...

106. This spacious new building was erected some time prior to the platform reconstruction and the old one was retained to the right, just out of the picture. It was used for parcel traffic mainly and has housed the signalling panel since 1981. (Lens of Sutton)

107. At 1.57am on 1st July 1906, the driver of the up boat train inexplicably entered the station at an estimated 67mph instead of the maximum permitted speed of 30mph. The high centre of gravity of class L12 no. 421 compounded the disaster, the locomotive rolling over on the 10-chain curve and hitting a goods engine (left), which prevented it falling into Fisherton Street. There were 28 fatalities and subsequently the speed limit was reduced to 15mph. In the 1920s, all trains were instructed to stop at the station. From May 1947, trains were allowed to pass through at 10mph, the limits now being higher. (Lens of Sutton)

108. The bay could be used for terminating local trains from the Basingstoke, Bournemouth, Bulford or Portsmouth lines. Class T9 no. 113 simmers in the evening sun on 19th July 1924, accompanied by the then inevitable milk churns. The ground signals had originally been fitted with rubber arms, to reduce injury to shunting staff. (H.C.Casserley)

109. The 8.25am Plymouth Friary to Waterloo departs from platform 2 behind no. 858 *Lord Duncan* on 17th June 1938. The rebuilt station was provided with a subway but this footbridge had been built in 1860, to provide a link with the adjacent GWR terminus. Although this closed in 1932, the footbridge remained until 1956. (J.R.W.Kirkby)

Salisbury Market House branch

110. The full length of the 460yd. long branch is shown on the map. The Salisbury Railway & Market House Co. was formed in 1856 by local businessmen who were frustrated by the remoteness of the proposed new stations from the Market Place and feared decline in the town's trade. The Market House was opened on 24th May 1859 and the line was worked and maintained by the LSWR, SR and BR successively. Cheese was carried until 1903, corn until 1913 and wool until 1940, although the track had been removed from within the Market House prior to WWI. Traffic ceased in 1962, the line was officially closed on 1st July 1964 and the company was voluntarily wound up in 1965. This view is from a train leaving platform 6 in April 1956, and includes a small platform (still existing in 1991) which served Main & Son, corn and seed merchants. Also on the right are the chimneys of the CEGB power station, which was then the terminus of the branch. Left of centre, a wagon stands in the siding of Building Materials Ltd., while the line's exclusive brake van stands near the malthouses, on the 1 in 60 gradient. (E.W.Fry)

111. The Market House, which was photographed in 1953, had 16,000 sq. ft. of working space and an internal steel gallery, with a goods hoist. Two of the three original bridges remain, as does the facade of the building, reminding visitors that the railway did once come to the centre of the city. The public library now occupies the site. (E.W.Fry)

112. The slender cast iron bridge at the rear of the Market House is seen in 1956. During WWII, tons of tinned corned beef had been carted over it as the building was used as an emergency food store. (E.W.Fry)

113. Viewed from the foreground of picture no. 109, class T9 no. 30730 stands at platform 1, waiting to leave for Portsmouth & Southsea, on 21st May 1957. On the right is the former GWR station, a listed building which was consequently still standing in 1991. (H.C.Casserley)

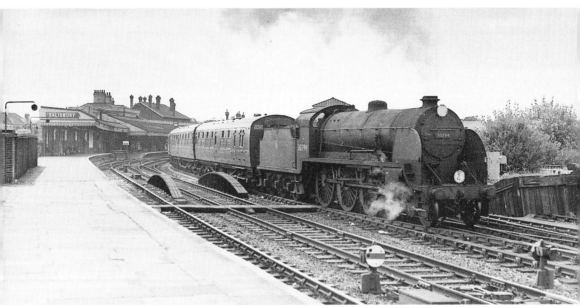

114. Viewed from platform 6 on 3rd August 1959, class N15 no. 30794 *Sir Ector de Maris* departs with the 3.15 pm semi-fast train, due to arrive at Waterloo at 5.32. Part of the ten inch diameter point operating air cylinder is visible. (J.N.Faulkner)

115. BR class 4 no. 76069 passes the 18 sidings of East Yard, hauling a cadet's special on 8th August 1964. A stone terminal was opened in this yard by Foster Yeoman in July 1987. On the right is the Market House branch and East Box, which was fitted with low pressure pneumatic equipment, shortly after Grateley. This was changed to the faster electro-pneumatic system in about 1935. This box, and the companion West Box, were the last on the Southern Region to use air power, both closing in August 1981. (J.N.Faulkner)

116. A 1965 photograph includes the former GWR refreshment room and water tank. The coaches at platform 1 were probably from the Bristol line. Since 1981, this track has been used for stock berthing and as an up freight reception siding, three through platforms being sufficient for passenger services. (C.L.Caddy)

117. No. D2291 was station pilot on 15th May 1965 and is probably bringing in empty stock from one of the five berthing sidings on the down side of the main line. These were still in situ in 1991, but seldom used. On the left is the milk dock, the site now being occupied by the British Rail Staff Association building. (C.L.Caddy)

118. Previously housed at Wimborne, Ambassador Exhibition trains occupied part of the former GWR site at Salisbury until early in 1991, when work started on a new depot for class 159 DMUs, scheduled to operate the route from 1993. No. 33001 leaves for Birmingham International with the 1984 Mid Wales Tourist Board Exhibition train, which included the Talyllyn Railway's 0-4-2ST no. 3 *Sir Haydn* of 1878. (C.Hall)

> **A map of the station before rebuilding and other photographs of Salisbury appear in our *Fareham to Salisbury* album, along with details of Milford Goods Depot. The GWR route and the line to Yeovil Junction will be featured in future albums.**

119. DEMU no. 1403 waits to leave from platform 6 at 19.44 for Portsmouth Harbour on 10th December 1984. Since then the speed restriction signs have been modernised and the potentially dangerous barrow crossing eliminated. Following the introduction of colour light signals in 1981, up passenger trains can start from platforms 2, 3, 4 or 6. (C.Wilson)

120. No. 33117 propels a 4TC set to Waterloo on 31st March 1989, this form of working having been introduced with the Bournemouth line electrification in 1967. Platform 4 accommodates not only most westbound services but on Saturday mornings (from March to December) it also has a bookstall specialising in railway publications and videos, which adds to the pleasure of those observing operations at this still important railway crossroads. (J.Scrace)

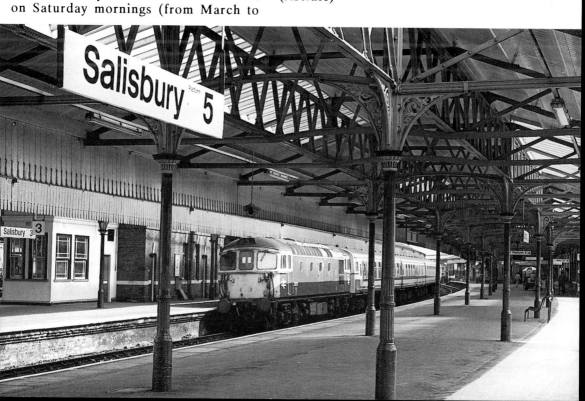

MP *Middleton* **Press**

Easebourne Lane, Midhurst. West Sussex. GU29 9AZ
(0730) 813169

Write or telephone for our latest booklist

BRANCH LINES

BRANCH LINES TO MIDHURST
BRANCH LINES AROUND MIDHURST
BRANCH LINES TO HORSHAM
BRANCH LINE TO SELSEY
BRANCH LINES TO EAST GRINSTEAD
BRANCH LINES TO ALTON
BRANCH LINE TO HAYLING
BRANCH LINE TO TENTERDEN
BRANCH LINES TO NEWPORT
BRANCH LINES TO TUNBRIDGE WELLS
BRANCH LINE TO SWANAGE
BRANCH LINES TO LONGMOOR
BRANCH LINE TO LYME REGIS
BRANCH LINE TO FAIRFORD
BRANCH LINE TO ALLHALLOWS
BRANCH LINES AROUND ASCOT
BRANCH LINES AROUND WEYMOUTH
BRANCH LINE TO HAWKHURST
BRANCH LINES AROUND EFFINGHAM JN
BRANCH LINE TO MINEHEAD
BRANCH LINE TO SHREWSBURY

SOUTH COAST RAILWAYS

CHICHESTER TO PORTSMOUTH
BRIGHTON TO EASTBOURNE
RYDE TO VENTNOR
EASTBOURNE TO HASTINGS
PORTSMOUTH TO SOUTHAMPTON
HASTINGS TO ASHFORD
SOUTHAMPTON TO BOURNEMOUTH
ASHFORD TO DOVER
BOURNEMOUTH TO WEYMOUTH
DOVER TO RAMSGATE

SOUTHERN MAIN LINES

HAYWARDS HEATH TO SEAFORD
EPSOM TO HORSHAM
CRAWLEY TO LITTLEHAMPTON
THREE BRIDGES TO BRIGHTON
WATERLOO TO WOKING
VICTORIA TO EAST CROYDON
EAST CROYDON TO THREE BRIDGES
WOKING TO SOUTHAMPTON
WATERLOO TO WINDSOR
LONDON BRIDGE TO EAST CROYDON

COUNTRY RAILWAY ROUTES

BOURNEMOUTH TO EVERCREECH JN
READING TO GUILDFORD
WOKING TO ALTON
BATH TO EVERCREECH JUNCTION
GUILDFORD TO REDHILL
EAST KENT LIGHT RAILWAY
FAREHAM TO SALISBURY
BURNHAM TO EVERCREECH JUNCTION
REDHILL TO ASHFORD
YEOVIL TO DORCHESTER
ANDOVER TO SOUTHAMPTON

LONDON SUBURBAN RAILWAYS

CHARING CROSS TO DARTFORD
HOLBORN VIADUCT TO LEWISHAM
KINGSTON & HOUNSLOW LOOPS
CRYSTAL PALACE AND CATFORD LOOP

STEAMING THROUGH

STEAMING THROUGH EAST HANTS
STEAMING THROUGH SURREY
STEAMING THROUGH WEST SUSSEX
STEAMING THROUGH THE ISLE OF WIGHT
STEAMING THROUGH WEST HANTS

OTHER RAILWAY BOOKS

GARRAWAY FATHER & SON
LONDON CHATHAM & DOVER RAILWAY
INDUSTRIAL RAILWAYS OF THE S. EAST
WEST SUSSEX RAILWAYS IN THE 1980s
SOUTH EASTERN RAILWAY

OTHER BOOKS

WALKS IN THE WESTERN HIGH WEALD
TILLINGBOURNE BUS STORY

MILITARY DEFENCE OF WEST SUSSEX
BATTLE OVER SUSSEX 1940

SURREY WATERWAYS
KENT AND EAST SUSSEX WATERWAYS
HAMPSHIRE WATERWAYS